BENJAMIN LIGHT

The Essential Christian Jokebook

A Treasury of Divine Humor

Contents

1

Disclaimer

While every effort has been made to ensure that the humor contained within this book is lighthearted and in good taste, we acknowledge that humor can be subjective and may not resonate with everyone. We understand that some readers may have more conservative sensibilities or preferences when it comes to comedy.

Therefore, we advise readers to approach the content with an open mind and a sense of humor. It's important to remember that humor is meant to bring joy and laughter, and while some jokes may push the boundaries of traditional humor, they are intended in the spirit of good fun and camaraderie.

We recognize that humor can be a sensitive subject, especially within the context of faith, and we respect the diversity of opinions and perspectives among our readers. Our goal is to entertain and uplift, and we hope that the jokes contained within these pages will bring smiles and laughter to all who read them.

If any joke inadvertently offends or causes discomfort, we sincerely apologize and encourage readers to skip ahead to the next section. Our aim is to create an enjoyable reading experience for all, and we appreciate your understanding and support.

Thank you for joining us on this comedic journey, and may your spirits be lifted by the joy and laughter found within these pages.

Introduction

H umor in the Bible is a nuanced aspect often overlooked amidst the serious themes and profound teachings. Yet, it is subtly woven throughout the text, enriching narratives and engaging readers. One prevalent form of humor in the Bible is wordplay, including puns and double entendres, which are particularly abundant in the Old Testament. For instance, the name "Isaac," meaning "laughter," humorously reflects the circumstances of his miraculous birth to elderly parents. Irony is another common element, seen in stories like Jonah, where the prophet's attempt to flee from God leads to unexpected outcomes, showcasing divine irony. Additionally, satire and absurdity feature prominently, as seen in Ecclesiastes' musings on the vanity of life, employing exaggerated scenarios to convey philosophical truths.

Understanding the humor in the Bible requires insight into its cultural context, rooted in ancient Israelite society and customs. Many jokes and humorous situations derive from everyday life, making them relatable to contemporary readers. For example, Elijah's taunting of the prophets of Baal on Mount Carmel involves sarcasm and mockery, reflecting cultural norms of the time. Moreover, humor serves diverse purposes, humanizing characters, conveying deeper truths, and challenging conventional thinking. Jesus often employed humor in his teachings, using parables and witty retorts to provoke reflection and challenge societal norms.

However, grasping biblical humor can be challenging due to cultural and linguistic nuances. Some jokes rely on idiomatic expressions or linguistic features specific to ancient Hebrew or Greek, posing translation challenges. Despite this, the humor remains relevant and resonant across time and cultures. By appreciating the humor in the Bible, readers gain insights into its messages and themes, fostering a deeper appreciation for its richness and complexity. Ultimately, biblical humor offers a unique lens through which to engage with scripture, revealing the depth of human experience and the enduring relevance of its teachings.

3

Humorous Moments in the Bible

Yes, there are several instances of humor and irony in the Bible, often reflecting human nature and the complexities of life. Here are a few examples:

1. **Abraham and Sarah Laughing (Genesis 18:9-15)**: When God tells Abraham that Sarah will have a son in her old age, Sarah laughs because of her disbelief. Later, when she overhears the visitors reiterating God's promise, she denies laughing out of fear, prompting God to question why she laughed.

2. **Elijah and the Prophets of Baal (1 Kings 18:20-40)**: In this story, Elijah challenges the prophets of Baal to a contest to see whose god will consume a sacrifice with fire. Despite their frantic efforts, the prophets of Baal fail, leading Elijah to mock them,

suggesting that their god might be sleeping or busy.

3. **Jonah and the Gourd (Jonah 4:6-10)**: After Jonah preaches to the people of Nineveh and they repent, he becomes angry at God's mercy. God provides a plant to shade Jonah, but then sends a worm to destroy it. Jonah's dramatic reaction to the loss of the plant highlights his misplaced priorities.

These examples and others show that humor is not absent from the Bible; rather, it offers insight into the human condition and the dynamics of faith.

4

Puns

Welcome to the delightful world of Christian puns! In this part of the book, we embark on a journey filled with humor, wit, and a touch of divine inspiration. Throughout history, puns have been a playful way to explore language and bring joy to everyday moments. Here, we apply this lighthearted approach to the rich tapestry of Christian themes, stories, and beliefs.

From the clever wordplay of biblical verses to the humorous observations of church life, Christian puns offer a unique blend of comedy and reverence. Whether you're a seasoned pun enthusiast or just dipping your toes into the punny waters, there's something for everyone in these pages.

Prepare to chuckle, groan, and maybe even facepalm as we dive into a collection of puns that celebrate faith, laughter, and the joy of sharing a good joke with fellow believers. So, grab your sense of humor and get ready to embark on a pun-tastic adventure through the world of Christianity!

1. Did you hear about the computer that went to church? It had too many "byte" sins.
2. Why did the tomato turn red? Because it saw the salad dressing!
3. Why did the pastor visit the beach? To test the "waters" of baptism.
4. How does Moses make his coffee? Hebrews it!
5. Why did the Bible feel tired? It had a lot of Psalms to get through.
6. What do you call a sleepwalking nun? A roamin' Catholic.
7. How did Adam and Eve feel when expelled from the garden? They were really "fruited" out.
8. Why did the Christian break up with his calculator? It didn't add up.
9. Why did the bicycle fall over? Because it was two-tired!
10. How do angels greet each other? Halo

5

Wordplay

S tep into the delightful realm of Christian wordplay! Within these pages, we'll dive into the playful world of puns, jokes, and clever linguistic twists that infuse humor and depth into the language of faith. From witty double entendres to ingenious wordplay, this section is a celebration of the creativity and joy found in the intersection of language and spirituality. So, let's embark on a journey of laughter and insight as we explore the humor and wisdom tucked away in the words of Christianity.

1. Why did the Christian break up with his calculator? Because it had too many sins (sines)!
2. Did you hear about the Christian chef? He beats eggs for breakfast and the devil for lunch!

3. How does Moses make his tea? Hebrews it!
4. Why was the math book sad? It had too many problems (mathematical equations)!
5. What's the best way to communicate with fish? Drop them a line from the Book of Jonah!
6. Why did the Christian teacher go to jail? For using too many Bible puns. It was a capital offense!
7. How does Jesus make his coffee? Hebrews it, of course!
8. Why did the Christian comedian bring a ladder to the show? Because he wanted to reach the highest praise!
9. Why don't they play cards on the Ark? Because Noah was always standing on the deck!
10. Why did the Christian athlete always win? Because Jesus is his coach, and he always plays to win!

6

One-liners

G et ready for an adventure into the world of Christian one-liners! In this section of our book, we'll explore bite-sized nuggets of humor that deliver laughs and moments of reflection in equal measure. From clever observations to light-hearted quips, these one-liners offer a glimpse into the lighter side of faith. So, buckle up and prepare to chuckle and contemplate as we navigate through a collection of witty remarks and amusing anecdotes that will leave you smiling and perhaps even pondering the deeper truths behind the laughter.

1. I told my kids I was going to pray, but I'm sneaking out to the living room to enjoy some heavenly snacks.

2. I asked the preacher if they had any books on trust. They whispered, "Would you believe they're right beside you!"
3. Why don't angels play hide and seek? Because they always find you when you're "praying"!
4. I asked God for a bike, but I know God doesn't work that way. So, I stole a bike and prayed for a good lawyer!
5. Why was the computer cold at church? It left its stained glass "windows" open!
6. My wife told me to stop impersonating an angel. I had to put down the wings.
7. I'm reading a book on miracles. It's impossible to put down!
8. I told my wife she should embrace God's missteps. She gave me a hug.
9. My dog used to chase squirrels a lot. It got so bad, finally, I had to take away his leash and pray for his obedience.
10. My Bible is so old, the Ten Commandments were originally in the "Ten Strong Suggestions" section!

7

Knock Knock Jokes

H old onto your hats, folks, because we're about to dive into the unpredictable world of Christian knock-knock jokes! But fair warning: these knee-slappers might just be too funny for comfort. Brace yourselves for a barrage of playful puns and hilarious wordplay, guaranteed to leave you in stitches. As you journey through this section of our book, be prepared for uncontrollable laughter and the occasional groan-inducing punchline. So, if you're ready to knock on the door of hilarity and step into a world where every knock leads to a hearty chuckle, then grab hold of your sense of humor and get ready for a wild ride!

1.

Knock, knock.

Who's there?
Isaiah.
Isaiah who?
Isaiah you later when I finish this joke!

2.

Knock, knock.
Who's there?
Esther.
Esther who?
Esther way to get to heaven?

3.

Knock, knock.
Who's there?
David.
David who?
David you know I'm a shepherd boy who defeated Goliath!

4.

Knock, knock.
Who's there?
Exodus.
Exodus who?
Exodus up to you to let me in!

5.

Knock, knock.
Who's there?
Noah.
Noah who?
Noah how to find grace in the eyes of the Lord?

6.

Knock, knock.
Who's there?
Jesus.
Jesus who?
Jesus loves you, that's who!

7.

Knock, knock.
Who's there?
Peter.
Peter who?
Peter the gate to heaven!

8.

Knock, knock.
Who's there?
Solomon.
Solomon who?
Solomon good Christian jokes!

9.

Knock, knock.
Who's there?
Timothy.
Timothy who?
It's the Timothy to pay your tithe

10.
Knock, knock.
Who's there?
Matthew.
Matthew who?
Matthew you will find, if you open the door

8

Observational Humor

W arning:

Prepare yourself for an abundance of laughter as we delve into the world of Christian knock-knock jokes! These rib-tickling anecdotes may just leave you in stitches, so make sure you're in a comfortable spot before diving in. From pun-filled punchlines to unexpected twists, these jokes are guaranteed to bring joy to your day. So brace yourself for some side-splitting hilarity and get ready to giggle your way through this uproarious collection of knock-knock humor!

1. Have you ever noticed how worship songs are like earworms? You hum one chorus, and suddenly it's stuck in your head all day. Praise God for catchy

tunes!

2. Isn't it funny how church potlucks always have that one dish that defies explanation? I mean, who knew there were so many ways to prepare Jell-O?

3. Have you ever noticed that every small group has that one member who always brings up the most obscure Bible trivia? I think they must have a spiritual gift in "random fact recollection."

4. You know you're in a Christian household when the fridge is full of leftovers from last week's fellowship meal, and you can't tell if it's the loaves and fishes multiplying or just good old-fashioned hospitality.

5. Ever wonder why the church bulletin is printed on paper that's seemingly impossible to fold back up neatly? It's like a divine test of patience before you even enter the sanctuary.

6. It's amusing how the church parking lot turns into a NASCAR track right after the service ends. Everyone's racing to beat the rush to the nearest restaurant for lunch.

7. Why is it that whenever the pastor says, "In

conclusion," you know you're in for at least another 15 minutes? It's like a spiritual version of bonus content.

8. Have you ever tried to find a Bible verse in the middle of a sermon and ended up lost in the Book of Numbers? Talk about divine direction taking an unexpected detour.

9. Isn't it ironic how the person with the loudest "amen" during the sermon is always the one who falls asleep right after the opening prayer? Maybe they're just resting their vocal cords for the grand finale.

10. You know you're a church kid when your parents threaten to ground you by taking away your Bible instead of your phone. It's the ultimate punishment and character builder all in one.

9

Situational Comedy

Prepare yourself for a journey through the hilarious world of Christian situational comedy! These jokes are not just about punchlines; they paint vivid pictures of everyday scenarios with a comedic twist that will have you rolling on the floor with laughter. From mishaps during church events to funny encounters with biblical characters, these jokes will surely tickle your funny bone. So get ready to chuckle your way through relatable situations and find humor in the everyday moments of Christian life!

1. Ever been in a church service where the person leading prayer forgets they're holding the microphone and suddenly starts narrating their inner thoughts? "Lord, please help Sister Sarah with her...

oh, sorry, didn't mean to broadcast that!"

2. Have you ever been in a youth group icebreaker where they ask everyone to share their most embarrassing moment, and you realize yours involves accidentally singing the wrong verse during a worship solo? Talk about hitting a high note of embarrassment!

3. Imagine being the one responsible for setting up the baptismal font before the service and accidentally turning the water temperature to ice cold. Nothing like a shock of cold water to wake up those seeking spiritual renewal!

4. Ever volunteered to be the designated driver for a church outing only to realize you're the only one sober enough to wrangle the rowdy choir members back onto the bus? It's like herding cats, but with hymnals.

5. Picture being the pastor giving a sermon on the importance of humility, only to realize halfway through that your zipper's been down the whole time. Talk about a lesson in practicing what you preach!

6. Ever been in a Bible study where the leader asks if anyone has any prayer requests, and you accidentally

blurt out your latest gossip instead? "Um, I meant to say, please pray for Sister Martha's cat, not her neighbor's drama!"

7. Imagine being the worship leader and accidentally hitting the wrong chord during the offering song, leading the congregation into a spontaneous rendition of "Amazing Grace" in the key of off-key. Now that's what I call an unexpected offering!

8. Ever been in a church fellowship where someone brings a dish they claim is "biblically inspired," but it turns out to be a questionable interpretation of manna from heaven? Who knew heaven's bread tasted suspiciously like burnt toast?

9. Picture being the children's pastor trying to wrangle a group of hyperactive kids during VBS and accidentally getting tangled up in the puppet strings during the puppet show. Suddenly, you're the star of your own slapstick comedy!

10. Ever volunteered to help with church cleanup day and accidentally knocked over the pastor's prized collection of antique hymnals? It's like a scene straight out of a sitcom, complete with the sound of crashing cymbals and shattered dreams.

10

Absurdism

G et ready for a wild ride into the realm of Christian absurdism! Absurdist humor thrives on the unexpected and the nonsensical, turning everyday situations upside down to reveal their absurdity. In this section, you'll encounter jokes that defy logic and challenge conventional wisdom, leaving you scratching your head and laughing out loud at the sheer absurdity of it all. So brace yourself for a journey into the wonderfully weird world of Christian absurdism, where the only rule is that there are no rules!

1. Ever wonder if Noah's Ark had a "No Humans Allowed" section for the animals to enjoy some peace and quiet during the flood?

2. Imagine if David's slingshot missed Goliath and instead hit the palace window, causing King Saul to accuse him of vandalism. "But Your Majesty, I was aiming for the giant, I swear!"

3. Picture Jesus turning water into not just wine, but sparkling grape juice instead. The disciples' reactions: "Um, Jesus, we were kind of hoping for something with a bit more kick..."

4. Ever ponder if the burning bush was just God's way of experimenting with a new BBQ grill design?

5. Imagine if the parting of the Red Sea caused a traffic jam, with the Israelites stuck behind a slow-moving caravan of camels. Talk about a divine detour!

6. Picture Moses coming down from Mount Sinai with not two, but three stone tablets, only to realize he miscounted and accidentally left out the eleventh commandment: "Thou shalt not lose thy car keys."

7. Ever wonder if the angels in heaven have their own version of a water cooler where they gather to gossip about the latest miracles and divine interventions?

8. Imagine if Jonah had gotten motion sickness

during his three days in the belly of the whale and had to ask for divine Dramamine.

9. Picture Jesus calming the storm on the Sea of Galilee, only for Peter to complain about getting seasick. "Lord, next time can we just take the scenic route through the countryside?"

10. Ever wonder if the manna from heaven came with an expiration date and if the Israelites had to deal with divine food poisoning? "Sorry, guys, I think I ate some expired manna yesterday. That's why I've been wandering in circles."

11

Humorous Bible Quotes

S tep right into the section filled with Humorous
Bible Quotes! Get ready to chuckle and
maybe even guffaw as we explore the lighter side
of scripture. From witty proverbs to amusing
anecdotes, these quotes offer a delightful glimpse
into the humorous side of the Good Book. So, without
further ado, let's dive in and discover some of the
funniest verses and passages from the Bible. Just
remember, even in the midst of laughter, there's
always wisdom to be found.

1. "And God said, 'Let there be light,' and then
suddenly realized He forgot to pay the electric bill."
- Genesis 1:3 (Parody)

2. "For I know the plans I have for you," declares

the Lord, "plans to prosper you and not to harm you, plans to give you hope and a future... unless you're trying to assemble IKEA furniture." - Jeremiah 29:11 (Parody)

3. "Trust in the Lord with all your heart and lean not on your own understanding, unless you're trying to assemble IKEA furniture... then just pray for a miracle." - Proverbs 3:5 (Parody)

4. "The Lord is my shepherd; I shall not want. But if you mess with His sheep, He'll find ewe." - Psalm 23:1 (Parody)

5. "Ask and it will be given to you; seek and you will find; knock and the door will be opened to you... unless you're asking for the last piece of pizza at a youth group sleepover." - Matthew 7:7 (Parody)

6. "Do not be anxious about anything, but in every situation, by prayer and petition, with thanksgiving, present your requests to God... especially if it's about passing a math test." - Philippians 4:6 (Parody)

7. "In the beginning was the Word, and the Word was with God, and the Word was God... but sometimes, the Word gets lost in translation." - John 1:1 (Parody)

8. "Love your neighbor as yourself... unless your neighbor plays the drums at 2 AM." - Mark 12:31 (Parody)

9. "And Jesus said to them, 'I am the bread of life. Whoever comes to me will never go hungry, unless you're on a diet." - John 6:35 (Parody)

10. "For God so loved the world that he gave his one and only Son, that whoever believes in him shall not perish but have eternal life... and free WiFi." - John 3:16 (Parody)

12

Jokes Written in the Style of Famous Comedians

Hey, comedy enthusiasts! Get ready to dive into the world of famous comedians with a Christian twist! From the classic humor of Jerry Seinfeld to the unique wit of Jim Gaffigan, we've got all the laughs you could ever want. So buckle up and prepare for a hilarious ride filled with humor, wit, and plenty of belly laughs. You won't want to miss out on this uproarious journey!

"Why, I remember when I was a kid, we used to go to church so often, I thought the pews had our names carved in 'em! And let me tell ya, the pastor had a sermon so long, he needed a commercial break! But you know, I still went, 'cause I figured if God can raise Lazarus from the dead, He can sure wake me up on a Sunday morning!"

· In the style of Rodney Dangerfield

Ever noticed how communion wafers are so dry? I mean, I took one bite and thought I was gonna need the wine just to wash it down! And don't get me started on those tiny cups! They're like shot glasses for saints! I'm telling ya, next time I'm bringing a water bottle and a loaf of bread, 'cause I need some hydration and a sandwich after that service!" *smash*

· In the style of Gallagher

What's the deal with manna? I mean, one day it's raining bread from heaven, and the next day, everyone's complaining about gluten intolerance! Is it just me, or does that seem a bit ungrateful? And speaking of complaints, have you ever noticed how the Israelites wandering in the desert were like the original Yelp reviewers? "Two stars, manna was bland, not enough variety, would not wander again!"

· In the Style of Jerry Seinfeld

You ever notice how the Bible's like the ultimate family drama? I mean, you've got sibling rivalry, parental favoritism, and enough drama to make even the Kardashians jealous! And don't get me started on the food in the Bible. It's like every meal is a potluck, except instead of Jell-O salad, you've got loaves and fishes. It's a miracle if you can find anything without unleavened bread!

· In the style of Jim Gaffigan

"Why did the Christian comedian bring a ladder to church? Because he wanted to raise the roof with holy laughter, kids! And remember, if laughter is the best medicine, then the Bible must be the ultimate prescription! Ha-ha!" - In the style of Krusty the Clown

13

Divine Remix

Welcome to the "Divine Remix" section, where we take your favorite pop hits and give them a heavenly twist! In this section, we're transforming well-known songs into hilarious Christian parodies. Get ready to laugh as we replace the original lyrics with biblical references and humor. From catchy tunes to timeless classics, these divine remixes will have you singing along with a smile on your face. So, let's dive in and enjoy the musical journey of faith and fun!

1. **"Wake Me Up Before You Go-Go" by Wham!**
   Original: "Wake me up before you go-go, don't leave me hangin' on like a yo-yo..."
   Christian Twist: "Wake me up before you go-go, don't leave me prayin' solo, Amen's the word, you

know..."

2. **"Sweet Home Jerusalem" by Lynyrd Skynyrd**
Original: "Sweet home Alabama, where the skies are so blue..."
Christian Twist: "Sweet home Jerusalem, where the scriptures come true, praise the Lord Almighty, hallelujah!"

3. **"Take Me to Church" by Hozier**
Original: "Take me to church, I'll worship like a dog at the shrine of your lies..."
Christian Twist: "Take me to church, I'll worship like a saint at the pew of your grace, my sins are washed away, hallelujah!"

4. **"Uptown Funk" by Mark Ronson ft. Bruno Mars**
Original: "Uptown funk you up, Uptown funk you up..."
Christian Twist: "Uptown praise you up, Uptown praise you up, we're dancin' for the Lord, Uptown praise you up!"

5. **"Don't Stop Believin'" by Journey**
Original: "Don't stop believin', hold on to that feelin'..."
Christian Twist: "Don't stop believin', hold on to

that faith in, Jesus, our Savior, He's comin' again!"

6. **"I Will Survive" by Gloria Gaynor**
   Original: "At first, I was afraid, I was petrified..."
   Christian Twist: "At first, I was lost, then I was crucified..."

7. **"I Want to Hold Your Hand" by The Beatles**
   Original: "Oh, please, say to me, you'll let me be your man..."
   Christian Twist: "Oh, please, say to me, you'll let me hold your hand, Jesus, lead me to the promised land..."

8. **"Stayin' Alive" by Bee Gees**
   Original: "Ah, ah, ah, ah, stayin' alive, stayin' alive..."
   Christian Twist: "Ah, ah, ah, ah, prayin' to survive, prayin' to survive..."

9. **"Happy" by Pharrell Williams**
   Original: "Because I'm happy, clap along if you feel like a room without a roof..."
   Christian Twist: "Because I'm saved, clap along if you feel like your sins are removed, hallelujah!"

10. **"I Will Always Love You" by Whitney Houston**

Original: "And I will always love you, I will always love you..."

Christian Twist: "And I will always love You, Lord, I will always love You, forever and ever, amen!"

14

Conclusion

In conclusion, "Christian Comedy Chronicles: A Hilarious Journey Through Jokes and Jest" has been a delightful adventure into the lighter side of faith. Through puns, wordplay, one-liners, knock-knock jokes, observational humor, situational comedy, absurdism, and humorous Bible quotes, we've explored the depths of laughter within the realm of Christianity.

From the humorous moments hidden within the Bible itself to the creative interpretations of modern-day Christian life, this book has celebrated the joy and camaraderie found in sharing a good laugh with fellow believers. We've laughed together at the quirks of church culture, the nuances of scripture, and the absurdities of life, all while recognizing the underlying truths and wisdom that humor can reveal.

As we close this chapter, let us carry with us the re-minder that laughter is a gift from God, a testament to our shared humanity, and a source of joy even in the midst of life's challenges. May we continue to find humor in the everyday moments, to share laughter with those around us, and to embrace the lightheartedness that brings us closer to one another and to the divine.

Thank you for joining us on this journey through the world of Christian comedy. May your days be filled with laughter, your hearts with joy, and your spirits with the ever-present love of God. Until we meet again, keep smiling, keep laughing, and keep spreading the good humor wherever you go. God bless!

15

About the Author

Benjamin Light, Ph.D. (Doctor of Divine Humor), is a theologian with a twist. Raised in a town where laughter echoed through the pews, he developed a unique appreciation for the lighter side of spirituality. With a knack for puns and a passion for comedy, Benjamin combines his academic insights with stand-up comedy chops to explore the intersection of faith and humor.

In "The Essential Christian Jokebook: A Treasury of Divine Humor," Benjamin invites readers on a rollicking ride through the world of Christian humor, celebrating the joy found in sharing a laugh with fellow believers. When not cracking jokes or analyzing scripture, you can find him hiking in the mountains or strumming tunes on his ukulele in his cozy cabin in the woods.

Benjamin Light 2024

Printed in Great Britain
by Amazon

50525478R00026